Many times, people feel that in order to redesign their life, it must be hard and difficult. Jill Whittamore proves that theory wrong and gives amazingly powerful and simple strategies that anyone can start right now to begin living life to the fullest. The questions and practices included within will have you looking at all areas of your life differently, and taking new and empowered actions to create the life you truly deserve. I wish I would have had a Pink Toolbox many years ago!

—Monica Kenton is a business and money coach, shaman, and author of Go Radical or Go Home: Be Spiritual, Make Money, and Change the World.

Use Jill Whitamore's *The Pink Toolbox* offers a variety of concrete ways to achieve your dreams and goals. In this concise book, Jill offers many proven tools that she and others have used to help people, especially single moms, working women and entrepreneurs, live a fulfilling life.

—Phillip Mountrose, co-creator of the online EFT (Emotional Freedom Techniques) Quickstart Kit, http://gettingthru.org

The Pink Toolbox is a must read for anyone who is looking for a simple straight-forward approach to real change.

—Shannon Burnett-Gronich, Conscious Living Publishing or Dare to Living Challenge

"Jill Whittamore is a healing force of nature. Her kindness, passion, and wisdom sets the bar very high for all teachers of truth, and it's been a great honor to share the platform with her."

—Mike Dooley, *NY Times* bestselling author of *Infinite Possibilities*

Testimonials

It has been about 1 year now since Jill came into my life. My mental and physical health is stronger, my outlook at the responsibilities that I have in my life have changed from one of frustration to one of joy. I am learning to relax and to let my guard down. It has been one of the best things I've ever given myself permission to do. Thank you Jill Whittamore-Coach ♥ you!-

C Johnson

Jill's sessions of Infinite Possibilities and further Coaching Sessions has really changed my life and helped me to be a better person in my personal and professional life.

I never did Visualization and Meditation techniques till I encountered the Awesome Jill. It has helped me to be calm and positive about my life situations in so many ways.

Huge Hugs and Thanks for being my Coach, couldn't have done a lot of this without you,

P Hartfield

You have been a valuable asset to me, in learning to deal with life's challenges in a positive way. Your unending, positive reinforcement helped me to focus on the good, and get my mind-set focused on the right things, and in the right place. I still think back on those lessons, and they never fail to help.

You're also a great role model... and I'm glad to have found you!

I highly recommend your services to anyone who's searching for positive growth and behavior changes in their lives.

Sincerely,
Fay M

THE *PINK* TOOLBOX

The Complete Book of Tools to Help Working Women Become Empowered and Transform Their Lives to Living Life on Their Terms

JILL WHITTAMORE

BALBOA.
PRESS
A DIVISION OF HAY HOUSE

Balboa Press books may be ordered through booksellers or by contacting:

Balboa Press
A Division of Hay House
1663 Liberty Drive
Bloomington, IN 47403
www.balboapress.com
1 (877) 407-4847

Because of the dynamic nature of the Internet, any web addresses or links contained in this book may have changed since publication and may no longer be valid. The views expressed in this work are solely those of the author and do not necessarily reflect the views of the publisher, and the publisher hereby disclaims any responsibility for them.

The author of this book does not dispense medical advice or prescribe the use of any technique as a form of treatment for physical, emotional, or medical problems without the advice of a physician, either directly or indirectly. The intent of the author is only to offer information of a general nature to help you in your quest for emotional and spiritual well-being. In the event you use any of the information in this book for yourself, which is your constitutional right, the author and the publisher assume no responsibility for your actions.

Any people depicted in stock imagery provided by Thinkstock are models, and such images are being used for illustrative purposes only.
Certain stock imagery © Thinkstock.

Printed in the United States of America.

ISBN: 978-1-4525-8532-1 (sc)
ISBN: 978-1-4525-8533-8 (e)

Library of Congress Control Number: 2013919276

Balboa Press rev. date: 11/19/2013

This book is dedicated to the single working women and aspiring entrepreneurs.

10% of the proceeds from this book are forwarded to national and local charities for the prevention, protection and support against violence against women.

Contents

Preface ix

Disclaimer xi

The Beginning 1

Values 4

Thoughts are Energy 10

Limiting Beliefs and Emotions 15

Affirmations 26

Visualization 28

Vision Boards 30

Meditation 31

Gratitude 33

Emotional Freedom Technique 34

Chakras 39

Forgiveness 42

Other tools 43

Emotions, Mood and Essential Oils 44

Final Thoughts 47

Preface

I created The Pink Toolbox to share the tools I use to significantly change my own life. I have manifested so many different things in my life, such as cars, trucks, vacations, relationships, career changes, prosperity, you name it I have manifested it.

The Pink Toolbox contains true stories and easy to understand instructions for all the processes I have used for many years. Best of all you can start using most of the processes immediately.

As a Board Certified Life and Holistic Health Coach I successfully work with clients on a one on one basis teaching the processes in this book. I decided I wanted to help more single moms, working women and entrepreneurs get out of their own way, exceed their goals and truly live the life they desire and to show women that they really can have anything and be anything regardless of where they are now.

The tools and processes in this book can be used by men, and teens, as well as women who want a positive change.

You must be willing to take full responsibility for your emotional and physical well being for the processes to work. You hold the power.

One of the obstacles I hear from women is they have been taught that living their life they way they want is selfish. The truth is it is not selfish it is selfless.

Disclaimer

The information in this book is based on my personal experiences and training as well as the experiences of many other clients and practitioners. It is for educational purposes and your personal use. Use of the tools and processes in The Pink Toolbox is your responsibility, not the responsibility of the author or developers. It does not represent medical advice from appropriate physicians or qualified practitioner.

It is always suggested to inform your physician of new modalities you will be trying.

Using EFT on behalf of others should comply with any state and country laws or licensing boards regarding such activities and is not suggested without thorough training and certification.

Meditations and visualizations etc. should not be practice while working with moving parts or driving any type of vehicle.

The Beginning

Life can be full of challenges. Between relationships, health, employment, finances and a myriad of things which can result in mental mayhem if you are not equipped with important tools to help you rise above, stay healthy and enjoy your life to its fullest. You can start living your life you dream of on your terms by living your life intentionally.

Our lives reflect the choices we make and the beliefs we have been subjected to through out our life. Wherever you are in your life today, you can change it to reflect what you truly desire. You do have to make the decision to stop living in mediocrity and invest time in yourself.

No one else is controlling you or can control you without your permission. You always have options and choices. Throughout "The Pink Toolbox" you will be given my personal stories to show you true-life examples of how the different "tools" have worked. The first story is below.

The first memory I easily recall with actively participating in choosing changing my life was when I was a freshman in high school. It was a new school in a new state. I wanted to reinvent myself from an overweight, unknown girl to a popular cheerleader. Thankfully my parents were supportive, my dad would even invite teenagers to come over for lunch so I got to meet people prior to the first day of school. School started and cheerleading signups began. The last time I tried out for cheerleading I didn't make the squad not even close and I felt embarrassed and had sworn I wouldn't attempt to be a cheerleader again. With that vivid memory how was I going to change my new life?

It took me a few days of self-talk, I had already signed up, I had to go through with it so, I started taking time out of my day imagining myself in those cute Black and Orange uniforms with the fluffy pompoms. It felt good so I added seeing me do cartwheels and splits and jumping up and down.

I kept acting as if I was a Tiger Cheerleader, everyone cheering for me.

The final day was here and they are naming the new Freshman Cheerleading Squad. I felt like throwing up and running for the hills (but wait there are no hills in Florida, well at least not in Cocoa). Guess what happened next? I hear Jill Minton please come up, what? Me? I did it! I was voted in. I was cheerleader and on my way to changing my teenage life.

I began to realize, I had power and I could change things I didn't like or want by changing the way I thought and seeing in my minds eye the way I wanted my life to be. At that age I thought I was the only one with such powers, but that is not true. Every single person on this earth can use their power of thought and visualization, meditation, EFT and the other tools in the Pink Toolbox to live the life they desire.

If fear is keeping you stuck where you are now and you have doubts that forward progress is possible and think it can't happen. It won't unless you make the choice to change your thoughts and start using the many tools.

I know that some of you can't imagine your life being different and want to change but you are scared, because if your life changes everything around you will suddenly start changing and at some point you may not recognize it at all. Just remember, it is okay to move forward and it is okay to be scared. We all get scared; we all have fears from time to time. Start taking the steps to change anyway. As a matter of fact picking this book up is one step and reading it is another step.

It is all in your attitude. No one has ever said that changing your attitude and your life is easy- at least at first. As you continue to read The Pink Toolbox and make the choice to change while taking steps every single day (yes even on the days you may not feel like opening your eyes) you will begin to see subtle changes and then more good things, sometimes they may even go un-noticed. This is why I ask that you use the worksheets in this book, use a journal and follow the exercises and stick to it if you want to live the life you design on your terms.

Side note- if you are not comfortable with writing or marking up a book than get a spiral note book or journal and do the exercises and record keeping in there.

So lets start!

I would like to ask you a question, most likely a question you have heard before. "If you could do or have anything in your life without the concern of money or any other obstacles what would it be?"

Why don't you have already?
When do you want it?
How do you want to live your life?
What is your idea of your perfect life?
Are you blocking yourself from getting it?

Don't worry if you are, it is hard to see when you are blocking your self.

I have got in my own way more times than I wish to admit, but that is one of the things that make us human. It is learning of your blocks, releasing them and moving forward that will change your life. There are still times when I find I am blocking myself. You will begin to be able to recognize this and be able to use your tools and begin unblocking yourself and moving forward. So lets do that- let us move on to the stuff that works.

One request, as you start using the daily tools, I suggest starting with one at a time, two at the most. This way you can tweak the processes so they will be as powerful as possible for you, as well as the more you use the tools, the more comfortable you will get and the easier it will be for you to stick with.

Values

I start most of my clients off with their current value system… do you know what they are?

Wikipedia defines a value as:

Personal **value** is absolute or relative and ethical value, the assumption of which can be the basis for ethical action. A *value system* is a set of consistent values and measures. A *principle value* is a foundation upon which other values and measures of integrity are based.

Some values are physiologically determined and are normally considered objective, such as a desire to avoid physical pain or to seek pleasure. Other values are considered subjective, vary across individuals and cultures, and are in many ways aligned with belief and belief systems. Types of values include ethical/moral values, doctrinal/ideological (religious, political) values, social values, and aesthetic values. It is debated whether some values which are not clearly physiologically determined are intrinsic such as altruism and whether some, such as acquisitiveness, should be classified as vices or virtues. Values have been studied in sociology, anthropology, social psychology, moral philosophy, and business ethics.

Values can be defined as broad preferences concerning appropriate courses of action or outcomes. As such, values reflect a person's sense of right and wrong or what "ought" to be. "Equal rights for all", "Excellence deserves admiration", and "People should be treated with respect and dignity" are representative of values. Values tend to influence attitudes and behavior. For example, if you value equal rights for all and you go to work for an organization that treats its managers much better than it does its workers, you may form the attitude that the company is an unfair place to work; consequently, you may not produce well or may perhaps leave the company. It is likely that if the company had a more egalitarian policy, your attitude and behaviors would have been more positive.

My definition is what makes you tick what makes you get up in the morning even if it is not going the way you dreamed and planned it would.

Below is a list of values you can use others if you like. I want you to pick 5.

Abundance	Contribution
Accomplishment	Control
Accuracy	Conviction
Adventure	Courage
Ambition	Creativity
Appreciation	Dependability
Artistry	Desire
Assertiveness	Diligence
Awareness	Discipline
Balance	Diversity
Beauty	Education
Belonging	Elegance
Boldness	Endurance
Bravery	Enjoyment
Change	Entertainment
Charity	Enthusiasm
Cheerfulness	Environmentalism
Clarity	Ethics
Clear-mindedness	Excellence
Commitment	Excitement
Community	Expressiveness
Compassion	Faith
Competition	Fame
Confidence	Family
Consciousness	Fidelity
Conservation	Financial independence
Consistency	Fitness

Focus	Organization
Fortitude	Originality
Frankness	Partnership
Freedom	Patience
Friendship	Passion
Fun	Peace
Generosity	Perfection
Giving	Perseverance
Grace	Persistence
Gratitude	Philanthropy
Growth	Playfulness
Guidance	Pleasure
Happiness	Popularity
Harmony	Power
Health	Practicality
Holiness	Professionalism
Honesty	Prosperity
Hopefulness	Punctuality
Hospitality	Recreation
Humor	Relaxation
Imagination	Reliability
Independence	Resourcefulness
Inspiration	Respect
Integrity	Responsibility
Intelligence	Self-control
Intimacy	Self-reliance
Intuitiveness	Serenity
Joy	Silence
Justice	Simplicity
Kindness	Sincerity
Leadership	Solitude
Love	Spirituality
Loyalty	Spontaneity
Making a difference	Strength
Mindfulness	Success
Open-mindedness	Teaching

Teamwork	Virtue
Thankfulness	Vitality
Thoroughness	Volunteering
Thoughtfulness	Wealth
Tranquility	Winning
Truth	Wisdom
Uniqueness	Youthfulness
Unity	

Write your top 5 values here:

_____

_____

_____

_____

Are you living them? _____

If so, write down how. If not, write why not.

_____

_____

_____

_____

What can you do to be in alignment with your values?

_____

_____

_____

_____

After all if one of your values is family time but you are not spending any quality time with your family because you are working 65 hours a week and the drive is long and when you get home the last thing you feel like doing is talking to anyone in your household or going for a walk with your family, guess what? You ARE NOT in ALIGNMENT.

Now, do you think you can change this?

I bet you say no…but the answer truly is YES.

I suggest every six months you recheck your values. See if they are the top values that make you tick. If not reassess. There are no wrong or right values. This is personal this is about you.

This is not what your mom, friends, sister, brothers or anyone else thinks your values should be. This is about YOU.

I will let you in on my top current values:

Happiness
Freedom
Health
Abundance
Love

Freedom has been one of my top values for a very long time. There was a time I was working Over 12 hours a day to prove myself to my boss, my kids and everyone else around me that had something to say about my life. When I was working like that every day I was a single mom on food stamps, and had Medicaid for my children's insurance. Working that much was not in alignment with my values and it showed up in many different ways such as added stress, lack of sleep, not spending time with my children, etc. When you are not living in alignment of your values you can begin to forget who you are and that you have the right exist in happiness without stress and in good health. I kept my thoughts and visions of prosperity and happiness, had faith that soon my life situation would change for the better, my hours reduced and more money and it did.

I check with my self all the time to make sure I am indeed in alignment with my own values.

One more important thing about values is you need to define for you what the values mean to you.

Example:

> Lets pick one of my values; Freedom. What freedom means to me is that I am not tied to the clock on a regular basis; it means I can come and go as I please, I do what I want when I want the majority of the time.
>
> The only limits on the definitions are the ones you put on them.

Thoughts are Energy

Simply put: to change your circumstances you must change what you're thinking. I am not simply talking about positive thinking. My suggestion is to pay attention to what your thinking and feeling.

Look around your life and begin to notice how your thoughts are affecting your life.

Thoughts are energy, everything is energy, even the chair you are sitting on is a form of energy.

Some people can see energy such as auras; chakras and some people heal with energy even at far distances.

Simply put, if you think negative thoughts, you will attract negative energy, and if you think positive thoughts will attract positive thought energy.

There are hundreds if not thousands of books that have been written and published on the subject of the power of positive thinking, you attract what you live, and The Law of Attraction, there are many different terms but essential it's the same thing.

The study of energy and like attracting like started very long before the 20th century.

Our thoughts are how we direct energy, so doesn't it make sense that if we can direct energy through thought we can change pretty much anything?

Knowing this I would think everyone would want to harness their energy and redesign their life as well as contribute to the good of all mankind and all universe.

Really think about this, if you control your own thoughts, your own energy doesn't that make you magical and powerful?

Until I started writing this book, I didn't really think about magicians and the "magic" they perform is it a hoax or is it using their thought energy to control their surroundings and the outcome of their magic trick?

Take a look at David Copperfield, who is the first living illusionist to be honored with a star on the Hollywood Walk of Fame. He has escaped from chains and shackles just before he was plunged over Niagara Falls, survived being locked in a safe inside an imploding building, making a daring "Escape from Alcatraz" prison, levitating and "Vanishing a 45 ton Orient Express Train Car" while surrounded by a ring of spectators, escaping while hanging upside down from burning ropes in straightjacket 10 stories above flaming steel spikes, testing his endurance by surviving the deadly heat standing in the center of a 2000-degree "Tornado of Fire", and flying through the air in "Flying." Is that proof about Thoughts being energy? What about Thoughts forming your reality?

The two quotes below were written thousands of years ago:

> Ask and ye shall receive. *Jesus*
> What you think, you become. *Buddha*

What do you think they are talking about? To me, it sure sounds to be like energy attracting like energy (which is basis of the Law of Attraction)

So do you use your thought energy in a light and positive way or negative and dark way? Or have you yet to harness your incredible power?

Quantum Physics proves that the Law of Attraction, (the energy of thought) works. And reality is a projection of your thought energy. Since everything in the universe is made of energy vibrating at different speeds and frequencies you attract at level you are vibrating.

If you are full of gratitude your vibrational energy and positive thoughts are going to give you more of that. If you are full of fear you will attract more of that.

Let me give you a few examples from my life.

I was engaged to a man in New York, I received information from my family that my dad had cancer. I was extremely upset- devastated in fact. I definitely didn't want to live in New York. My dad needed me I need to be closer. I was leaving New York one -way or the other. Everyday placing all of my thought on leaving NY and returning to Florida. I began looking at houses in Florida, cutting pictures out of magazines. Telling everyone I was moving.

Then my fiancé announced we would be buying a home in Florida and he would visit every few weeks. *REALLY? This is too good to be true!* So we found a piece of land and a contractor, applied for and received a loan. Construction on our new home had begun.

I would visualize my new home, all the details right down to the placement of the trees and the flowers. What could be better it was on a lake in a brand new community. Next thing you know I am back in Florida, looking at and walking in to my brand new home, on a lakebed with a pool. I spent my days and nights working on the home. Alas, everything is in place.

The trees are growing the pool is done, the mirrored living room walls, and the white silk couch I wanted. All the colors in all the rooms just perfect just as I visualized.

There were other people who didn't think it was as perfect as I; they say the lake as a dry lakebed. Your Reality is how your perceive it. This means the way you observe something or think about it will affect the outcome of a scenario. Different people view the same situation differently at the same or different times may look very different to each "witness". That's why the situation that you find funny might be completely depressing to another.

Think about your life and your perceptions. Are there areas of your life you would like to change?

Start with what you are thinking about most often. So where does your thought energy call home? How about the way you perceive your current conditions.

Trust me- you can change them from negative to the positive.

From a life of lack to a life of positive abundance. It truly is your choice and you have the power to change it.

Start with your thought energy and your perception. This does take a lot of commitment to you

If you are always saying that you need to get out of debt, do you know what the universe is going to do? Keep you right where you are full of debt in other words the universe takes the thought as oh ok you want more of "get out of debt"!!

Another example would be a conversation like this: "How are you today?" and you answer "ok, I am just so tired" or "okay but I wish I didn't have to go to work today" Do you know what you're going to get? Being more tired and always wishing you didn't have to go to work"

As one of my favorite Authors and Speakers states Mike Dooley says: "Thoughts Become Things"

You have to choose your thoughts and words wisely it might be strange or even a little difficult for you at first but it gets easier and easier as you are choosing positive thoughts and feelings it becomes a habit and a way of life. As it does you will see so many great things transpire in your life. If this is a new concept for you my advice is to start small with things that are believable to you. So you need to get a handle on your thoughts, feelings and take action.

If you wish to eliminate fear, concentrate on courage. If you wish to eliminate lack, concentrate on abundance. If you wish to eliminate disease, concentrate on health. If you wish to get rid of hate, concentrate of love. Do you get the picture? Don't concentrate on what you don't want or don't have instead concentrate on what you do want to feel and experience. If you concentrate all your energy on what you don't want that is what you are going to get more of.

Always concentrate on the ideal as an already existing. In other words live your life with full and complete intention. If you are wanting to be a Architect than research what it takes to be one, find out what the majority of them do when not working, find what the similar connections are, where they like to eat etc. and start mimicking it. I am not saying be fake or fraudulent. What I am saying is to start participating in the same or similar activities and keep working towards your dreams. If they wear fitted grey suits- then go to a tailor or store that fits men or women in suits. Keep going keep acting as if you already are whatever it is you want to be or live where you want to live.

If perhaps after awhile of acting as if, or going to meetings with other "architects", and the "Grey Suit" you have decided that isn't what you want than that is okay too, at least you got to experience being an architect.

Give some thought about what you might want to try next! There are no limits only the limits you put on yourself.

Limiting Beliefs and Emotions

Limiting beliefs are the obstacles that keep you where you are and won't let you be where your dreams take you. A limiting belief is a belief which stops you from moving forward. It lives in your subconscious most of the time. Sometimes a limiting belief is so deeply wedged in your subconscious it may take months and months or more to remove and release. Limiting beliefs can come from your upbringing (even as a very young child), your culture, and your peers what you see on TV. Limiting beliefs are also why some people do not believe you can create your own reality because those beliefs are getting in the way of your manifesting.

These beliefs are there to protect you in a strange sort of way. But they keep you in neutral and sometimes even in reverse. These beliefs are self sabotage and must be destroyed. If you find yourself repeating the same sentence all the time, you should realize that it's a belief that you have. Start paying attention to your negative talk and your negative thoughts and write them down. Read them out loud if you begin to get feel badly you know you are recognizing the destructive belief and can begin on the path do destroying that belief. When certain things in your life seem to happen again and again and you don't want them to this is also a way a limiting belief shows up in your life.

If you have a limiting belief that mistakes are bad, then you'll avoid making a move because your too scared to make a mistake; therefore you won't grow. It doesn't make a difference where your influences came from, your parent, aunt, uncle, anyone that you spent time with in your life and left an impression. Maybe they used to say things as money is hard to earn, Money doesn't grow on trees, I cannot afford this right now etc. In their defense they had no idea it would show up in your sub conscious and have a huge affect on your adult life.

I suggest limiting your media time, there are tons of negative subliminal message invading your subconscious every day from commercial ads on TV, radio to billboards, let alone the negative things you hear and see all over the news.

This is where the affirmations, forgiveness, gratitude, EFT, visualization and meditation will come in and we will cover that in detail a little later.

You can read all the books in the world and spend every waking hour researching but if you don't take action – you can have all the book knowledge but still stay in the same stuck place going nowhere or backwards. Everything requires devotion, emotion and action to succeed. So just start.

Exercises to get you thinking

What are your first 5 negative limiting beliefs or obstacles?

1.

_____

_____

Do you know where it came from?

_____

_____

What would be a belief you would rather have?

_____

_____

2.

_____

_____

Do you know where it came from?

_____

_____

What would be a belief you would rather have?

_____

_____

3.

_____

_____

Do you know where it came from?

_____

_____

What would be a belief you would rather have?

_____

_____

4.

_____

_____

Do you know where it came from?

_____

_____

What would be a belief you would rather have?

_____

_____

5.

_____

_____

Do you know where it came from?

_____

_____

What would be a belief you would rather have?

_____

_____

The Exercise below will help you sort out where you are now and where you want to be.

EXERCISE:

What do you think about your job/career?

_____

_____

_____

What would like to be doing?

_____

_____

_____

What can you do to work towards this?

_____

_____

_____

Do you like where you live?

_____

_____

_____

Jill Whittamore

Where would you like to live?

_____

_____

_____

What do you think about money?

_____

_____

_____

What do you think about rich people:

_____

_____

_____

Why?

_____

_____

_____

What do you think about your appearance?

_____

_____

_____

What do you think about success?

_____

_____

_____

What is success to you?

_____

_____

_____

How is your social life?

_____

_____

_____

How is your heath?

_____

_____

_____

What would you like to change in your life?

_____

_____

_____

What is the first thing you want to change?

_____

_____

_____

Why?

_____

_____

_____

When do you want to make changes?

_____

_____

_____

Write down the first small steps you can take towards your first change:

_____

_____

_____

How will your life be different once this is changed? In other words what will that part of your life look like?

_____

_____

_____

Will this affect anyone else? If so, how?

_____

_____

_____

What is the second thing you want to change?

_____

_____

_____

Why?

_____

_____

_____

When do you want to make changes?

_____

_____

_____

Write down the first small steps you can take towards your second change:

_____

_____

_____

Jill Whittamore

How will your life be different once this is changed? In other words what will that part of your life look like?

_____

_____

_____

Will this affect anyone else? If so, how?

_____

_____

_____

What is the third thing you want to change?

_____

_____

_____

Why?

_____

_____

_____

When do you want to make changes?

_____

_____

_____

Write down the first small steps you can take towards your third change:

_____

_____

_____

How will your life be different once this is changed? In other words what will that part of your life look like?

_____

_____

_____

Will this affect anyone else? If so, how?

_____

_____

_____

Once you made your first three changes. List the second set if changes you are going to take.

When you have successfully made your changes and/or reached your goal please start this exercise again with your next set of 3 things in your life you want to change, improve have control over and continue to repeat the exercise in bite size pieces.

Affirmations

An affirmation has been said to be a form of prayer that focuses on a positive outcome. I see affirmations as being good to yourself and changing your vibrations to a higher frequency. Positive affirmations can help develop a powerful and positive attitude to life. A positive outlook is essential in your life to succeed and be in good health. I love affirmations you can say them in your head but the best way is to say them out loud. Leave yourself notes on your fridge, mirror, anywhere. You say your affirmations daily and they can change depending on what it is you are trying to create.

This is an example of an affirmation:

I am love
I am self-confident
I am full of joy
Every day in every way I am becoming more self empowered
I now accomplish all my goals effortlessly
I am proud of my abilities

Here are other affirmations:

Courage:
I am proud of who I am; I respect myself
I am strong, courageous and in control of my life
I find it easy to approach & communicate with others
I act with bravery in all situations
I find it easy to draw upon inner strength and courage

It's easy to speak my mind, and I do it
Day by day, in every way, I build my strength and courage

Prosperity:
I deserve to be prosperous and I accept it now
I give myself permission to be prosperous
Money comes to me easily.
I surround myself with positive, loving people
I am open to receiving & happiness and abundance

You can make your own affirmations to suit your particular needs. You can record your own affirmations and save them to your phone. You can buy affirmations created by other people.

If you find that you are having a difficult time believing the affirmations you can change them to something you can believe easier and simply change them as you go. There are no rules- other than use them every day and don't give up.

There is also what could be called negative affirmations also known as complaints. Watch yourself with complaints, they are negative thoughts you put out and since like attracts like your creating a low vibration, energy and thought and will get it back in return.

Visualization

Visualization is a must in helping you change your life. Visualizing is the process of placing pictures in you minds eye as detailed as possible and feeling how you would feel if it were true. You can visualize anything you are trying to attain.

How to visualize:

Make yourself comfortable. Lie down or sit up, spine straight

Take a slow, deep.

Continue to take slow, deep breaths.

Start to see in your minds eye what it is you are wanting.

Feel it use your every sense to make the visualization more powerful. See it, smell it, taste it, feel it.

Visualize for 5-10 minutes a day.

You can visualize more than once a day but not suggested more than twice.

The more emotion in the visualization, the more power you are putting to your dream and letting the energy escape into the universe so it can best suit your desires. Not only is this an effective way to make your dreams reality but also it is a lot of fun.

I have used this tool to get a new car, recreate my life time and again, go on trips, start relationships, and create abundance. You name it; you can use it for everything.

A word of warning we are all here with free will, it is an universal right, be ethical and do not try to manipulate others. If you are trying to create a relationship use details. List all the attributes you are looking for in a mate but not a specific person. Other people have the same opportunities to create the life they choose.

Vision Boards

What is a vision board? A vision board is also called a Dream board, Treasure Map, a Visual Explorer or Creativity Collage; new names are always popping up. It is typically a poster board on which you paste, tape or collage images that you have cut out from various magazines or downloaded from the Internet. You can add your own text, designs anything that will help you to feel the joy when you are looking at your board. Vision boards can be cork boards, screen savers, anything that you will see throughout the day and feel good.

Similar to visualization you surround yourself with images of whom you want to become, what you want to have, where you want to live, where you want to vacation, anything and everything you desire.

Before you begin your vision board it is best to sit quietly, set your intent ask yourself what you would like this vision board to be. Be open to any ideas that come to you.

There are different types of vision boards, vision boards that are general with not too much thought behind it which is one where you simply pick pictures that you like, there are vision boards that you intentionally choose pictures to obtain a particular goal, career. There are no rules, do what makes your feel good.

The Law of Attraction states the we attract into our lives anything that we give attention regardless whether it is positive or negative. Surrounding yourself with pictures of things or events that make you feel good will help you attract it.

We have what is called Reticular Activating System, which is an information filtering system. Vision Boards aide with external stimuli that can help us get closer towards our desires.

Meditation

Another tool I use and highly suggest everyone uses is the practice of meditation.

Sometimes I feel meditation gets a bad rap because people assume you have to sit still for 45 minutes, be a vegan and dress differently. None of which is true.

I suggest to all of my clients that they start off slow. No more than five minutes a day to begin, but try doing it every day. Find a time and place that is convenient for you this will make it easier for you to stick with it honestly—just do it. Five minutes to start.

Once you are comfortable and in the habit of meditating then increase to 10 -20 minutes a day and on days when you have the luxury then 45 minutes.

There are several different types of meditation practices you can try such as:

* Vipassana, it's about letting your mind go and accepting whatever thoughts come up, while being detached from each thought.
* Zazen is seated meditation in the Buddhist tradition, but in the modern, it is done for long periods of time, you sit with your back straight. There is no attempt to change the breath.
* Transcendental Meditation you sit with your back straight Lotus posture, and use a mantra, is repeated. Your focus is on rising above all that is impermanent. It focuses on the breath and changes the breath to change one's state of being.

You do not need to start out concerning yourself with what type of meditation your are going to practice. My advice is to start simple and not worry about the label attached to the meditation.

You can try a silent meditation (which may be the hardest at first) or a guided meditation as well as musical meditations. I have a few on my website as well as you can go to you tube and try different variations out at no cost. (At least at the time of writing this You Tube is still free to use.)

Find out what works for you now – don't concern yourself with anything or anyone else's opinion—this is for YOU. This is your clearing time, your quiet time.

You may want to use a yoga pillow, eye patches to keep out light.

Meditation has many benefits including health benefits such as:

- It lowers oxygen consumption.
- It decreases respiratory rate.
- It increases blood flow and slows the heart rate.
- Leads to a deeper level of relaxation.
- Good for people with high blood pressure as it brings the B.P. to normal.
- Reduces anxiety attacks by lowering the levels of blood lactate.
- Decreases headaches.
- Builds self-confidence.
- It increases serotonin production which influences mood and behavior
- Helps in chronic diseases
- Reduces Pre- menstrual Syndrome.
- Enhances the immune system.

I also consider Yoga to be a form of meditation. It strengthens your mind, body and soul connection. I use yoga on a daily basis. I fit it in wherever I am. You can try simple poses or a complete routine. As with the rest of my suggestions start simple and let it become a habit. Then if you want to change the complexity, go for it.

Gratitude

There is a lot to be said about gratitude, I make a point before I even get out of bed in the morning I find at least five things I am grateful for and I say them out loud. At the end of the day I write down things I am grateful for. You can be grateful for what is right in your life, or even a cup of coffee it doesn't matter. The more grateful and thankful you are the less anything else matters.

Choosing and developing an attitude of sincere and "heartfelt gratitude for all that you have now unleashes the power for receiving even more. Being grateful is a positive vibration and since like attracts like you will continue throughout your day with positive vibrational energy. Every Day Give Thanks.

My suggestion is before you ever get up out of bed in the morning find at least 5 things you are grateful for; if you get stumped then use the save five you did yesterday. Be grateful you're your health, or your fingers, your bed anything and everything.

The important thing is that you are grateful and you feel grateful for what you already have- when you are in the consciousness of being grateful your future wants are a non-issue.

This is another very important habit because you begin to train your mind to think well thoughts and be thankful which oozes out positive energy and positive thought which in turn gives you more of the positive energy and vibrations.

I also suggest a gratitude journal that your write in at the end of the day and list a minimum of 5 things you are grateful for that happened today or that you were gifted with today; be it a creative thought, a phone call—you get the picture

Emotional Freedom Technique

Emotional Freedom Technique also known as EFT or Tapping is based on the energy meridians of Chinese acupuncture. EFT was brought to light in the 1970's by founder Gary Craig and continues to gain respect through positive results. Almost anyone can perform EFT you do not need special equipment or need to be in a special location or special time of day. EFT can be very fast, it is flexible. All you need is your breath, your index and middle fingers and your sincere intent.

It was once thought that your brain couldn't change after the teenage years, but it can be changed at any age. New Neural connections can be formed. When something triggers a negative emotion new neural pathways are created and they can be triggered and retriggered again and again. So negative emotions and limiting beliefs don't go away they fester and may get even worse. EFT/Tapping interrupts the creation of the negative neural connections, in turn encouraging the limiting beliefs to be released. Below is the basic recipe/short sequence most practitioners' use. Different practitioners use different points and some don't tap on certain points while others do. This is what I am comfortable with.

First- find and name the emotion/habit/pain you want to change. One very important note to this first step is that in order for EFT to work you have to really "feel" the pain or emotion. Let the pain/emotion exist in its most powerful form. If you are just stating the issue but do not allow the negative feeling your success will be minimal if at all. I believe this is one of the biggest reasons people are unsuccessful and give up on EFT.

Second- Find the intensity. In EFT the intensity is called the SUDS level that means Subjective Units of Distress Scale. The scale is from zero, which is no intensity to ten, which is extreme intensity. Pick a number, it doesn't have to be exact just pick a number and go with it.

Third- Write down the SUDS level.

Fourth- Start tapping on your soft spot (see diagram) that is located about four inches down and under your collar bone or you can tap on your karate spot. You will start with your affirmation that will be using such as "even though I have this _____, I still love and appreciate myself. If that doesn't feel right use something that does such as even though I have this, _____ I will try to accept my self or I am trying to be all right with it. Tap on your spot and repeat the affirmation out loud three times.

Five-The reminder phrase, you will tap on all points using your reminder phrase which will be a shorten version of your affirmation and it can change as you go. Let's say your affirmation is "Even though I have this hurt, I still love and appreciate myself", the reminder phrase may be as simple as "this hurt". Tap through the top of your head, eyebrow point, outside eye corner, underneath the eye, under the nose, the chin, collarbone, and lastly under the arm. Repeat twice and reassess your SUDS level- write it down.

If when you reassess you are at a zero great job. If not but your SUDS is at 2 or below do two more rounds of tapping if you feel the need to change the affirmation and reminder phrase then please feel free to do so. If it is higher you may want to do also do 2 more rounds of the short sequence tapping. If after your second round of tapping and reassessing your SUDS level and your SUDS level hasn't changed to a lower number you may want to consider the longer tapping sequence that includes your fingertips as illustrated. If you have no change you need to tune in more, there also may be a need to clear yourself of any toxins such as caffeine, sugar, alcohol, processed foods etc. There is one more change that may have occurred which is your emotion may have shifted. Perhaps it started as embarrassment now it is anger. This is normal, change your affirmation to the new emotion, evaluate the

SUDS level, do your affirmation, tap on your sore spot or karate chop point while stating your affirmation three times and continue to do two rounds of tapping. Always take a deep breath when you are done with the rounds. Sometimes you may take a deep long breath in the middle of tapping this simply means your energy is moving.

If tapping doesn't seem to be working there may be several reasons why, such as mentioned before toxicity, your environment, having perfumes on, you may even need to change location.

There is also a long tapping sequence if you can not get your SUDs level to a zero. You would tap the Gamut point, which is located on your hand just below your knuckles in between your pinky and ring finger, while stating your issue. There is also an eye roll added which you look up, to the right side, the left side and then down without moving your head.

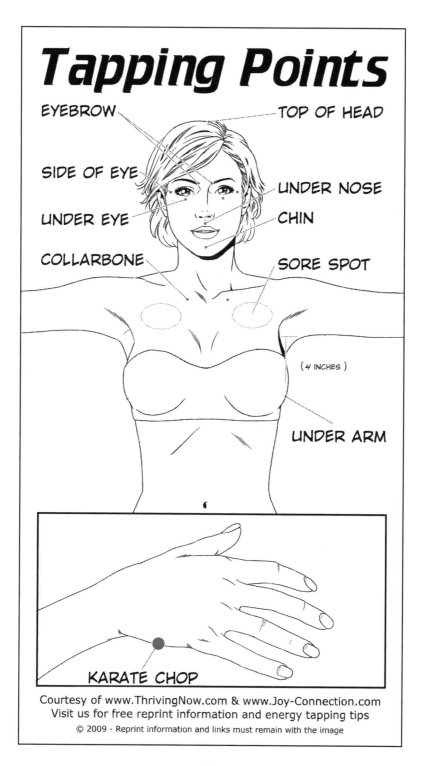

Tapping Points

EYEBROW

TOP OF HEAD

SIDE OF EYE

UNDER NOSE

UNDER EYE

CHIN

COLLARBONE

SORE SPOT

(4 INCHES)

UNDER ARM

KARATE CHOP

Courtesy of www.ThrivingNow.com & www.Joy-Connection.com
Visit us for free reprint information and energy tapping tips
© 2009 - Reprint information and links must remain with the image

37

Finger Points

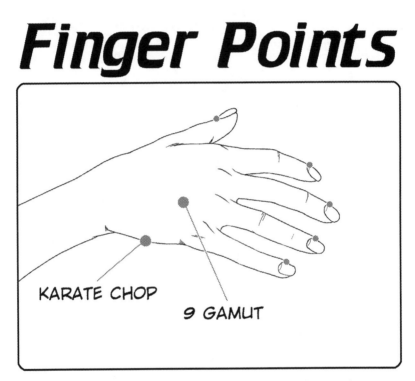

KARATE CHOP

9 GAMUT

Courtesy of www.ThrivingNow.com & www.Joy-Connection.com
Visit us for free reprint information and energy tapping tips

Chakras

"Chakra" means "wheel of light" which refers to the motion of energy within the center.

Our body has seven primary chakras. They regulate our physical, emotional, mental and spiritual states of consciousness. There are many aspects that are shared between the energy systems and physical organs. There are many disagreements as to whether there is a right or wrong way for your chakras to spin. My opinion is as long as they are bright and not broken in your minds eye than it doesn't matter because chakras are your own personal energy system and since every human is different it only makes sense that the spinning motions will also be personalized from being to being.

Personal story: I was on a cruise once and I landed up on the floor unable to get up due to the massive pain in my back. After taking pain pills and anti-inflammatories like sugar I was able to get up. I continued to spend weeks and weeks in massive pain and using the toxic solutions of today's society. After Ct Scans and MRIs and physical therapy I was diagnosed with broken bones in my back. What that meant was inevitable back surgery and pain medicine for the next 75 years of my life. That was not an option so I decided this was time to use my tools (that I had forgotten about like most people tend to do). I began to work on my first and second chakras as well as using visualization. The end result is I am strong and healthy. I pick up my grandchildren, move furniture, exercise and live my life in a normal fashion. The point of this paragraph is to show you that you REALLY can heal yourself.

Let us start with a brief description of our Chakra system:

Your first chakra is your grounding root chakra, which is a bright ruby red light located at the base of your spine. It affects your adrenal glands, appendix, bones, colon, kidneys, legs, knees and ankles. It is your connection to the earth and survival of money, safety, self-confidence and security. If you are feeling fear, over indulgence, anger, aggression, you will need to work on this chakra through visioning it bright and glowing through your front and back body spinning.

Second chakra your sense of being orange chakra located in your lower abdomen in your navel area. This chakra affects your bladder, intestines, lower vertebrae, pelvis, reproductive system and urinary tract. This is the chakra for freedom of self, cultural power and primal relationships. It is also associated with blame, guilt, power, jealousy, and sexual dysfunction. You will heal this by concentrating on a bright orange light full and not broken or ripped, shining through your front and back body.

Third Chakra is your self-empowerment chakra. This chakra is bright yellow and affects your gallbladder, digestion, liver, mid-back, nervous system, spleen and stomach. It is associated with intimidation, worry, seeking approval, nervousness. To mend this energy see in your mind's eye a bright healthy, whole yellow light spinning through the front and back of your body.

The fourth chakra is your heart chakra, which is green with a tinge of pink. This chakra effects love and joy. The heart chakra affects your blood, breasts, heart, circulatory system, lungs, lymph nodes, upper back and skin.

The fifth chakra is the throat chakra is a blue chakra located in the throat area it is sky blue. This fifth chakra affects your arms, hands, mouth, throat, neck, shoulders, thyroid and more. If you are having issues with judgment, humiliation, criticism, denial, and suppressed expression than you need to work on this chakra.

The sixth chakra is the "Third Eye" or brow chakra which in the center of your forehead between your eyebrows. The color is indigo. The central nervous system, inner ear, left eye, upper sinus, pituitary gland and hypothalamus are all affected by this energy center. If you are confused, or having nerve disturbances, depression or self doubt try working your third eye chakra by visualizing a very strong indigo light. Look for anything like inconsistencies or rips in the chakra or anything else that may need repair and repair it in your inner world.

The seventh chakra is the crown chakra located at the crown of your head (top of your head). The color violet and white is related to your spirituality, humanitarianism, trust and universal access. This chakra affects your brain, central nervous system, pineal gland and cranium. If you are having issues with the inability to trust, self consumed, guilt, depression try envisioning a violet light penetrating your front and back body, imagine it bright and full.

There always seems to be an emotional energy reason for physical pain trusting in your mind, body and soul connection really can heal you. It isn't usually overnight but you can heal. I am not in any way telling you to stop taking your prescriptions, physical therapy etc., that your doctor(s) have suggested; but I feel confident that if you start using the tools and processes included in The Pink Toolbox you can improve on your current situation. I do suggest keeping a journal of your journal it is very easy for us to conveniently forget where we were and deny any improvement- it is human nature.

Forgiveness

Forgiveness is extremely important because if you hold on to animosity, feelings of anger you are holding on to negative vibrational energy. As you learned earlier in this book negative vibrational energy attracts the same negative energy so unless you change the energy you are going to remain in a downward negative vibrational spiral and the person that is being affected the most is you!

Change your vibration and forgive. You do not have to make an elaborate gesture. Write a letter of forgiveness, pick up the phone it doesn't matter your vehicle of forgiveness, just do it. When you do you will feel like a ton of bricks has been lifted from you, your energy will change and you will be in a space where you can receive. When you forgive you are releasing not only the other person you believe to have wronged you but you are releasing yourself.

You can also tap on forgiveness also. First using the way the person made you feel and go through each emotion one at a time until all of the aspects of your anger and hurt have gone.

This is not to say you wont remember what happened, but when it does come up will not have the emotional charge that it did in the past.

Other tools

There are many other avenues you can use to help as you transform your life.

Feng Shui which works with energy and the placement of furniture, the colors you use and wear, shapes, etc. Crystals to help heal and protect, Reiki, Qigong, Tai Chi.

I also use binaural beats which according to the Monroe Institute is when two coherent sounds of nearly similar frequencies are presented one to each ear with headphones. The brain integrates the two signals, producing a sensation of a third sound called the binaural beat. The binaural beat is neurologically conveyed to the reticular formation that uses neurotransmitters to initiate changes in brainwave activity.

Brain Waves & Consciousness
Beta:(13-26 Hz) Alert concentration and problem-solving
Alpha (8-13 Hz) Alert relaxation
Theta (4-7 Hz) Deep relaxation and increased learning
Delta (1-3 Hz) =deep sleep

You can investigate Binaural Beats (for free at the time of writing) on You Tube as well as other sites. Most of the time you want to use the binaural beats when you are not driving and fully awake.

Emotions, Mood and Essential Oils

With all the fun, abundance, gratitude and joy in our lives we all still experience difficulties at some point in our lives sometimes it feels like a test and how we respond to the challenges is part of our emotional environment. The more you are aware of your emotions and strengths the easier it will be to be able to still see the joy, abundance and love in your life even during the difficult situations. Even with a strong mind and a lot of support, you may need additional tools to use to help you through rough territory.

Essential oils can help with our emotions, lift our spirits as well as be used for preventative medicine, acute and chronic illnesses. You can use essential oils for cleaning,

I became an oil consultant to be able to offer my clients an alternative to over the counter and prescription drugs. When I became an essential oil consultant my experience has been eye opening. The oils I use work, but they are pure oil. One of the reasons I didn't like oils in the past was because they didn't smell good for the most part and didn't do anything else. Come to find out the reason for this is because most commercial companies are allowed to label their oils in such a way that makes you think they are pure, but they are not. An essential oil can be labeled 100% pure as long as there is 10% pure oil, so what that means is there is 90% of a bunch of "stuff".

Working with essential oils, giving classes, watching webinars and finding out what has worked for my clients has lead me to include the oils in this toolbox because they really work and are not toxic. Did you know that essential oils entire your blood stream in less than 30 seconds? Think of all the substances you have put on your skin that have travel to your blood stream. It is kind of a scary thought.

On the next page I am going to list some essential oils that work with your mood and emotions. The list can be found on essentialoilme.com, this is a fantastic resource for ailments and oils this site lists protocols, research and testimonials.

If you are interested in the oils I use you can contact me. For respect of my readers I am not advertising any brand, but my warning is get the oils as pure as you can find. Read the entire label. Most of the oil labels will state "Not for Consumption" or "Not for Internal Use". Think about it though, if you can't use the oil internally than it is not pure. If an essential oil is made directly from the plant you should be able to use it internally.

The list below is from Dr. David Hill; I have used the oils myself and have used them on clients for emotion and mood adjustment.

- Acceptance - Balance, Elevation
- Anger - Balance, Grapefruit, Patchouli, Serenity
- Change, dealing with - Citrus Bliss, Serenity
- Courage - Balance
- Emotional foundation - Citrus Bliss, Elevation, Serenity
- Emotional protection - Frankincense
- Emotional release - Geranium highly recommended plus Basil, Cassia, Cypress, Melissa, On Guard
- Feminine Energy - Ylang Ylang or Sandalwood
- Forgiveness - Balance, Serenity
- Grief - Balance, Elevation, Geranium, Serenity
- Honesty - Purify
- Joy - Elevation or Citrus Bliss
- Motivation - Elevation
- Nurturing - Ylang Ylang or Serenity
- Paranoia - Bergamot, Breathe, Terra Shield, Vetiver
- Passion - Citrus Bliss, Elevation
- Reinitialize - Balance, Citrus Bliss
- Responsibility - Balance, Aroma Touch, Balance/Vetiver

- Self Confidence - Balance, Frankincense, Frankincense/
  Peppermint, Balance/Vetiver
- Self Image - Serenity
- Self Love - Balance, Serenity

Many suggest using single oils or a blend in a roller bottle and applying it behind the ears, on the wrists or on the bottoms of the feet 2 or 3 times daily. Others simply rub 2 - 3 drops on the palms of the hands and cup them over the nose and inhale deeply.

Another technique for the application of the oils is suggested by Dr. David Hill. of doTERRA CPTG Essential Oils recommends a light massage action along the spine and applying the oils to in regions that are in close proximity to the sources of blood flow to the brain. He also specifically mentions the areas of the right and left jugular just below the chin on the front and each side of the neck. The other is the suboccipital triangle, which not only gives proximity to arterial flow to the brain but also key neurological tissue. He describes finding this by placing the fingers on the sub occipital protuberance (little bump at the top of the spine on the back of the neck) then just below this grip the large muscle tissue and roll the fingers off to the side. This depression just behind and below the ear is the suboccipital triangle is suggested to be an excellent place to topically apply these oils and blends.

You can use the essential oils in a diffuser, on your skin (test for sensitivity first), cotton ball and most of doTERRA pure essential oils you can ingest them for acute and chronic illnesses as well as preventative medicine.

Final Thoughts

I hope you have already begun using the processes in the Pink Toolbox book. Remember, life is a journey, not a destination and not a race. You are here by choice and are meant to be happy and make not only the best of your life, but you are meant to be successful and abundant.

Abundance is different to everyone. So don't walk around with a tape measure trying to see if you "measure up" to the next person or your best friend. Abundance can be a tent in the forest for some or it can be free time with the family for others.

As you learn to live your life with intention this doesn't mean that you are not ever to experience sadness, difficulties or a negative experience. When you move through a difficult experience it is most important to be grateful for what you have experience in your life so far. This is the most important time to use your tools to help you through and to learn any lesson you are meant to learn. Never give up and never stop believing in love, happiness and success.

Life is meant to live and live it well, so go out there and live your life to the fullest. If you find that family or friends are not supportive of you or are making fun of what you are trying to do than at least in the beginning you are going to need to steer clear of them as much as possible this isn't forever, just for a little while. Their opinion and negative thoughts will go away as you become the person you are meant to be and live the life of your dreams. It is catchy, your friends and family will see you happy, calm and abundant and want to learn your secret. Share your joy and knowledge with those whom are open to receiving, it will have a ripple affect that can essentially change the world in which we live.

If you are looking for further support do not hesitate to contact me. I continue to work with clients on a one on one basis as well as workshops and group sessions.

Sign up for my weekly newsletter, special offers and events at any of the following:

www.helpwithhappiness.com
www.thepinktoolboxbook.com
www.doterra.myvoffice.com/jillwhittamore

Printed in the United States
By Bookmasters